When the Temple Burns, the Door to E-phe-sus Opens

This Episode is dedicated to my children, Fae of the highest and deepest order who lean into the wind no matter what power tries to defeat them.

"Fairy tales are never thought out [i.e., invented];
they are the final remains of ancient clairvoyance,
experienced in dreams by human beings who still had the power.

    Rudolf Steiner, ON THE MYSTERY DRAMAS
    (Rudolf Steiner Press, 1983), p. 93.

"Among them were many who had preserved in large measure the heritage of the old dim clairvoyance
— the intermediate state between waking and sleeping.
Such men knew the spiritual world from their own experience and could tell their fellow-men of what goes on there.
In this way there arose a world of stories about spiritual beings and events.
The fairy-tales and sagas of the peoples came originally from these real experiences in the spirit."

    Rudolf Steiner, OCCULT SCIENCE - AN OUTLINE
    (Rudolf Steiner Press, 1969), p. 219.

    It has been some time since I have put pen to paper on a labour of love such as this. And I doubt I could revisit any of my seminal work or influences between the year 2000 and now – June, 2016 – that did not speak to this piece in some obvious and tangible way. As has been said recently, all of my energy has been converted and it is to this end that I ride at a full gallop.

I am here to speak of the Fae, or the Phe, Fe, or Fey. The first spelling I prefer for its beauty. The first spelling I sense is about those entities wedded to the earth so very, very long ago…those entities being brought to a more material consciousness rather quickly now and with a force as the enemy is engaged. One might think that the enemy is being engaged on the material, in this hologram, and that is so. However, we are engaged in battle on dimensions outside our conscious understanding and in ways we might not even recognize as battle. There is ample evidence in realms we depend on such as etymology, mythology, archaeology, astronomy and esoteric research to make quite a compelling case for the presence of the Fae as a primary seed race.

When I speak of the Phe, I tend to mean those who came from a planet not so far away, in the Big Dipper or the Plough, likely during the period of about 5000 years ago at the transition between Lemuria and Atlantis. These were the seed race for the modern human being, the Sidhe and the hybrids. These were also, I suspect, the etheric teachers of the Lumerians. More will be said about these later. The Lhas. There will be, I suspect, a real temptation to confuse these beings with the archons and the archontic infection. However, there is ample evidence that the archontic infection originated in the area we now know as Israel and Palestine and it manifested itself much, much later.

When we write about the Fe, we are also writing about iron, for Fe is the alchemical and chemical symbol for such. Iron and the so-called fairies of legend are bound inextricably. However, there is a grave misunderstanding here. Those who wedded themselves to the earth are, in fact, of a virginal and pure nature and can be seen as the eyes of the earth in the granite and in the metals. The granite, of course, is a real part of the earth. The metals are, as well, but the metals are alien. They are not 'earth,' but rather they are singularities. Noble and pure. The eminent esoteric scientist and philosopher, Dr. Rudolf Steiner, speaks of these and in association with these, of deep wells from which, if we are not confused by the light, we might see the stars even in the daytime.

There is also the yearly Perseid meteor shower and the traditional acknowledgement of iron being sent to us from outer space for strength. This legend is generally carried forward by the idea of the Archangel Michael hurling iron toward the earth for strength against the Dragon. Phe vs. Draco? Perhaps. Is iron the protection from fairies or the protection of the Fae? Or is this iron assault every autumn an assault on the Fae/Phe themselves from elsewhere? These are fascinating questions.

Finally, when we speak of the spelling Fey, we speak of deceit perhaps. It is in this spelling, this Spell, that we find the negative Fey. There are those who perhaps carry an infection? It is perhaps something akin to the artificial separation of the two brain hemispheres: completely unnatural and forced. Fae from Fey. I often write and speak about an artificial intelligence, one that would create but can only copy, an unenlivened mirror image of the original. This perhaps is the Fey aspect. However, this is an intuitive speculation on my part. The intense insistence on separating the human brain spheres in our age, however, is all too real.

The title of this episode is extremely important to me personally. The day I finished writing *The Sun Thief*, also a labour of love albeit an extremely painful one, my house on Temple Street burned to the ground. Rudolf Steiner sent a message to me via people I trusted: when the temple burns, the door to Ephesus opens. He had said that originally when his beloved first study centre, the Goetheanum, burned to the ground. Since then I have held that thought not knowing completely what it meant, just that Ephesus was a Mystery School.

Steiner also noted that those within the Mystery School of Ephesus came to understand after the burning of their Temple that what was written in the flames, as it were, was a sort of 'jealousy of the gods,' and that, indeed, they needed to understand and acknowledge that there were 'gods' and that they were jealous of any further advancement of humanity. What the acolytes at Ephesus had been learning was the true secret of the Word. It is the combination of breath, warmth and liquid…that from which a human is made and with which a human 'makes.'. It is also, as I have said in lectures discussing the elementals, the space where weather occurs. Controlling the weather, as seems to be the frenzied, demonic goal of the geoengineers and soldiers, may mean an attempt to control the Word. The Word, after all, is how we manifest via the Sacred Imagination from the Morphogenic Field to the material plane, our own enlivened hologram. Manifesting happens via sound, the oral histories are the authentic histories, and so forth. The 20th century obsession with changing the frequency we bathe in should be considered a critical clue, as well, to where our power resides and to what the Predator is after. The Word resonates via the human Voice and the Vocal Chords thrum to a vibration and frequency.

Much has been written and told through the ages about the Fae. This presence itself has never been questioned and always been with us. The characterization has evolved but essentially we have always been accompanied by tales of fairies and changelings and such. In my mind, it seems the Fae have almost always been intermingled and confused with the elementals and other Nature Spirits. The Fae are something else altogether, most closely depicted by JRR Tolkien in his Middle Earth characterizations. The tales, as with all tales like these, do tell us the exact nature of the phenomena. However, we lose the authenticity of it, the tales become 'fairy tales,' fantasies, whimsy and imaginings. Relegating the Imagination to a place of diminishment has reduced this part of our history to the realm of cobwebs we sweep out of the corners of nurseries. (It is important to note that one reason it is extremely difficult to do any research on the Fae is that, over and above the mythologizing of such, many fantasy games have developed since the era of Dungeons and Dragons which include a hefty helping of Fae fantasy and so one can only get as far as those discussions generally). This is about to change, I imagine. The Fae are. They are within and without. They/we are inextricably wedded to this earth and everything naturally living upon her. We cannot be easily pushed aside or dismissed, if at all, and the other non-terrestrial races are well aware of this.

This is why any trace of validity having to do with 'fairies' has been shattered. It has been a matter of survival for the rest. Let me explain…

Moving on, let us say that my Temple burned. Then someone, an initiate I work with, told me that I am a pure Fae bloodline. Then I came across the works of Erhard Landmann who wrote of the reality of the Phe as they come from the planet Phecda in a constellation just between us and Ursa Major. Once these things started to come to me, I was able to take every post-it note I attached to my body this time around and place them, one after the other, in an indisputable validation of both my heritage and a validation of what was being said by Landmann in Germany.

The Phe are. They are both an alien race active within the manifestation of the modern earth and an ancient race deeply wedded to the material and spiritual substance of our planet. The first question, of course, that anyone would ask is where is the proof? Other than having a photograph taken with a member of the otherworld Phe, which I have not got…yet…I can say that to my mind the proof is in the location of the planet in a constellation which appears to rotate around our own pole star in the shape of a swastika. The swastika is one of the most ancient positive symbols extant in the ancient world. We can discuss that later in the episode. Regarding attempts to study the planet itself, I discovered much to my dismay that the word *phecda* is some sort of slavic slang for call girl. In fact, that does not surprise me. The overriding gesture of the Fae is feminine and the church has been hiding Mary Magdalene behind the lie of prostitution for some time. It is an old trick to keep us from investigating the truth and to keep us focused on a False

Masculine rather than the Sacred Feminine and Sacred Masculine..

The subject of the Fae in a written evaluation came to my attention via an article from Erhard Landmann, a German IT Specialist who is 85 years old now and unwell. He has made a deep study of the Fae or Phe in his lifetime. I suppose one way to gain attention for this seed race is to immediately attach oneself to this idea of abductions. Landmann was quite interested in that. There is a long association with this idea of Fairies (the mythology generated over time regarding the Phe), and abductions whether it be FE-tuses or children or adults. I have recently been told of abductions in Ireland, lasting for a day or two, in which the abductee was replaced into this world in a field famed for its fairy inhabitants. So this is still happening but the question is what are these modern abductions really and in what way are they potentially related to the Phe?

I will include the transcript of Landmann's article, noted in italics, translated into the English, here in this episode peppered liberally with my analysis. Landmann's work is absolutely vital to this study, to the world, and to me personally. If one speaks German, his videos can be seen on youtube lecturing on various matters.

Landmann's work relies almost exclusively, and quite successfully, on etymology. Etymology is both a lost art and somewhat vulnerable to change and so it is quite important to safeguard the lines of genesis of meaning. However, most important in his work is not necessarily the etymology (although that is critical in some ways) but the sheer frequency of basic Fae connected words combined with

geography and meaning. Truly, this is the Art of Etymology! The history of words and parts of words, shed of superimposed cultural changes absolutely rampant in the last hundred and fifty years, will tell us every truth we need to know .I have come to understand a few things at the moment about the Fae (I interchange that spelling, which is more feminine, with Phe, which points to the home planet). The Fae are lots of things. My own personal bloodline is 100% Fae, for example. This is why the military, I am told, tried DNA splicing with my genetic material when I was seven years old and, happily, were unsuccessful. T'was not the first I heard of the Fae in connection with myself. In fact, in mid-October, 2014, in Berlin, it seems I was visited by such and examined…particularly my heart…to make sure I was 'alright.'

The surname of St. Louis, associated with Louis IX of France, yes, but also the fleur-de-lis of the French court, is then a symbol for the Fae bloodline on the male side. The beautiful, curling leaves one sees often on the coat of arms of many names, such as one of the names of my maternal line, Almond, signals the Fae line on the maternal side. The Almonds were also deeply Masonic. I believe the maternal was of the York Rite and the male was of the Scottish Rite. They married then landed in Corpus Christie, Texas, in the mid-1800s. The heraldric emblems are just a bit of the open secret nature of our Fae heritage as human beings. The St.Louis family immigrated to Ireland just at the time of the French Revolution. The other French blood ancestors, that of Pierre Chastain, left France around 1695, and eventually landed in Virginia in 1700.

Interestingly, there is a 'Fae' family crest. Some have said it belongs to Morgan le Fey, the legendary sister of Arthur Pendragon. That is debatable. However, I am including it here because I have heard an analysis that indicates the 'animal' depicted on the crest is a wolf and the wolf is the sign of the Clan Mothers and so this would indicate the severing of the Fae from the Clan. I have grave doubts about that. I see the animal as a dragon. I see the Fae and Draco as mortal enemies, in a way. Certainly, the Draco faction currently trying to bring about the complete subjugation of our planet are not going to be excited about a resurrection or acknowledgement of a race that has a critical dual purpose: one of which is to shepherd the earth itself in the Middle Realms. Therefore, when we examine the

following crest, I see a dragon head pierced by a sword. There is also some research, presented later, that the Fae guided the Lemurians as they made the change from Lemuria to Atlantis and left behind a nature that was deeply astral or animal. This sword through the animal could also speak to that.

      The Phe are also interstellar creatures who come from the planet Phecda and, those who lived here for eons as a seed race, literally joined with the planet and act as shepherds and guardians. Also, as noted, Tolkien wrote about the Fae, or certainly what he thought were the Fae in his *Lord of the Rings* trilogy. It is a good thing to delve into Tolkien's research on the matter, if one can. This is one of unfortunate modern situation in which so many fantasy games have been generated based on humanity's everlasting affection for the Fae that the truth is hidden under the game. Like the changing of the meaning of the word phecda, this is another common ploy for making research difficult.

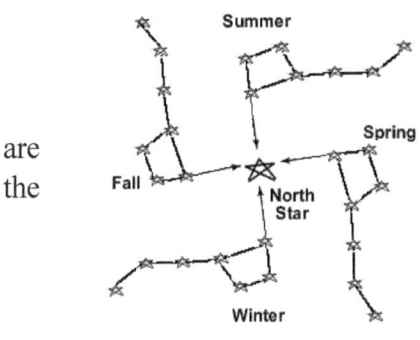

are the

Indeed the Fae have connected to or are originators of the Atlantean race. The planet itself can be located at the bottom left corner of the Big Dipper (the Plough). It is circum-polar, meaning it appears to revolve around the North Star, Polaris, yearly. And, when it does, it forms one of the most ancient and powerful symbols known to man, the swastika. This I noted in the introduction. It cannot be emphasized too much.

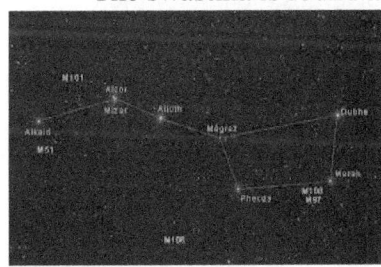

The swastika is found all over the planet in the most ancient milieus. It is one of the primary pieces of evidence in my view that supports the proposition that the Fae/Phe are one of, if not the, primary seed races. Consider the following :

This is a Middle Neolithic pottery vessel created more than a thousand years before the earliest of the Chinese states arose. What then means the swastika in the center square? Have you ever wondered why the swastika is a symbol found in the art of the vast majority of cultures in the northern hemisphere? This particular photograph displays the shape of ancient Chinese cities and their relationship to the number 9. That may or may not be considered in this particular discussion. It is an important factor for me personally. However, in light of the above mention of the Dragon and the Fae on a crest with a sword through a Dragon Head, it is very much worth mentioning that the Chinese refer to Ley Lines as Dragon Lines. There is also a Dragon Line tradition in Britain. The Irish refer to the ley lines as Fairy Lines.

Also, a semi-hidden tale of the Fae as Seed Race is found in the bardic tale of The Battle of Moytura. They appear to be, at the time of this writing, the Tuatha de Danaan. This links quite well the Fae with the ancient Celtic Hearth. The TdeD came from elsewhere to Ireland. The Danube River, one I just crossed this weekend for the first time this lifetime, fairly whispers magic at me regarding the Fae and the Celtic Heart. The Danube…the de Danaan…Dana, and so forth. In the tale of the Battle of Moytura, a race is described as coming from the water, the Fomora. There are ley lines called water lines. And, again, in Ireland, the ley lines are also referred to as Fairy Lines.

"Irish people claim that the first teachers of their race came not from the east from Europe but from the west and that ancient robed priests came out of the ocean on the west coast of Ireland and that these were the ones that instructed them. The Irish have a considerable folklore dealing with Atlantis." (Manly P. Hall).

The Battle of Moytura took place roughly in the area where Sligo exists today on, indeed, the west coast of Ireland. The bardic tale says that the Fomora came from over the sea or from under the sea. The met the current inhabitants, the Fir Bolg, but then were face-to-face with the Tuatha de Danaan, also invaders of Ireland.

After we take a close look at Erhard Landmann's article, I would like to bring the idea of the transition between the Lemurian and Atlantean incarnations of this planet into a bit more focus and just how this tale of the Battle of Moytura could be describing this evolution. The article itself is here in italics with my notes in plain print.

Who is behind many of the UFOs abductions?
By Erhard Landmann

(translated from the German by Joska Ramelow)

I would first like to present a series of facts that appear to have no connection at first sight. For thousands of years there have been tales of fairies and they are so deeply ingrained into different languages that the word "fairy tale" is equated with tales about fairies, as in French ("Contes de Fee") or English ("Fairytales"). Interestingly, since the timeline presentation of 'history' or themes in Waldorf education is the recapitulation of history…the first grade or class one topic is fairy tales. The First. Fae. I will write more about Rudolf Steiner as seems appropriate through this article.

In Spain, Portugal and along the French Atlantic coast, they have the story of the "white ladies", "Dames Blanches", "Damas Blancas". For centuries, more precisely since the takeover of power by the Catholic Church, these apparitions have been interpreted as the appearance of Mother Mary, in order to control these unusual events.

In French mythology, **Dames Blanches** (meaning literally **white ladies**) were female spirits or supernatural beings, comparable to the White Women of both Dutch and Germanic mythology. The Dames Blanches were reported in the region of Lorraine (Lotharingen) and Normandy. They appear (as *Damas blancas*, in Occitan), in the Pyrenees mountains, where they were supposed to appear near caves and caverns. There is a deep tale of a portal near there, very deep. It was recently written about by a woman called Patrice Chaplin. She asserts that she has been into this portal and leads others to and into it. These portals are considered to be fatal to humans in nature except for a very fortunate few who manage to get in and get back out. According to Chaplin, these portals are connected to Renne-les-Chateau. For my purposes, I care only about the ley lines, the portals and the potential connection to the Fae, both the inter-dimensional Fae and those married to and at one with the planet.

Thomas Keightly (1870) describes the *Dames Blanches* as a type of Fée known in Normandy "who are of a less benevolent character." They lurk in narrow places such as ravines, fords, and on bridges, and try to attract the attention of passersby. They may require one to join in their dance or assist them in order to pass. If assisted she "makes him many courtesies, and then vanishes." One such Dame was known as *La Dame d'Apringy* who appeared in a ravine at the Rue Quentin at Bayeaux in Normandy, where one must dance with her a few rounds to pass. Those who refused were thrown into the thistles and briar, while those who danced were not harmed.

There are many, many of these legends which include the famous Lady of the Lake who was associated with Marlin and was caretaker of a famous sword, which she bestowed upon the rightful king, Arthur. A sword is one of the four instruments of power always with the Fae.

J. A. MacCulloch believes *Dames Blanches* are one of the re-characterizations of pre-Christian female goddesses, and suggested their name Dame may have derived from the ancient guardian goddesses known as the *Matres* by looking at old inscriptions to guardian goddesses, specifically inscriptions to the *Dominæ*, who watched over the home, perhaps became the Dames of mediæval folk-lore. I contend that these are not a re-characterization of any entity but rather simply another story of a Fae interacting with a human.

The Dames Blanches have close counterparts in both name and characterization in the neighbouring northern countries of Germany and Holland.

The **Matres** (Latin "mothers") and **Matronae** (Latin "matrons") were female deities venerated in Northwestern Europe from the first to the fifth century. They are depicted on altars that bear images of goddesses, depicted almost entirely in groups of three, that feature inscriptions (about half of which feature Continental Celtic names and half of which feature Germanic names). Information about the religious practices surrounding the Matres is limited to the stones on which their depictions and inscriptions are found, of which over 1,100 exist. The Germanic Matres have been connected with the later Germanic disir, Valkyries and norns attested largely in 13th century sources.

The *Aufanian Matronae* (detail) from the Gallo-Roman temple site at Nettersheim in Bonn. They have been called also the 'august nurses.'

When one journeys back to the Norse myths and the 3 Norns, managing their cauldrons and the fact that we use these three for past, present and future…the cauldron in Norse mythology is spit into by Odin. The cauldron is the larynx. This is the words. The matrons go to the Dames Blanches and these are all the Fae.

The Stream of the Sacred Feminine and the Fae and the searing attack through the ages on the same! The attack on the feminine in the 20th century made children deeply vulnerable. To get the children away from the Divine Feminine is interesting in light of this tale of the fairies stealing children. That has to be sorted out.

This idea of appearing in white matters as well. White is virginal, after all. Pure and incorruptible. Philosopher Rudolf Steiner described the granite at the top of the Swiss Alps as virginal, as being in essence the eyes of the planet looking out (as were crystals). The appearance of the women in white lends itself to this imagination of virginity or purity at any rate and frankly the reason Steiner brings up granite in that environment is that it is pure. Look for us in the pure rock of the earth? In the metal which is clearly different from stone/earth. It is the becoming one with the earth that matters. And a more material consciousness now for good reason that it is in the rising to our aid and the aid of the planet mother.

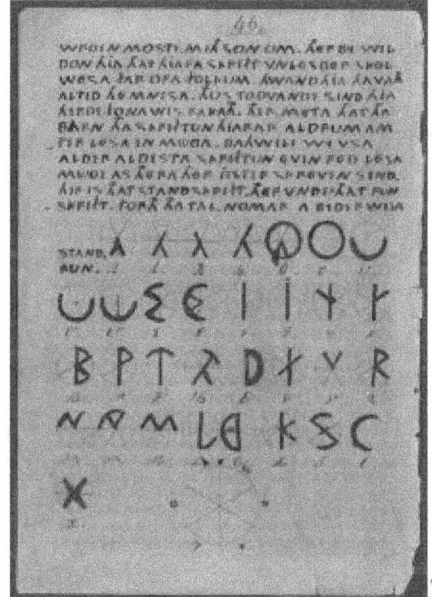

The Oera-Linda-book[1] mentions the ancestor Fraya, who gave birth to the first man into this world without being preceded by an act of sexual procreation, which was consequently later termed

"the immaculate conception of Mary" by the Christian Church. The Voynich – Manuscript[2] displays many naked women on dozens of pages. We have reports of tens of thousands, if not hundreds of thousands of abductions by so-called UFOs, where men are forced to engage in sex with women

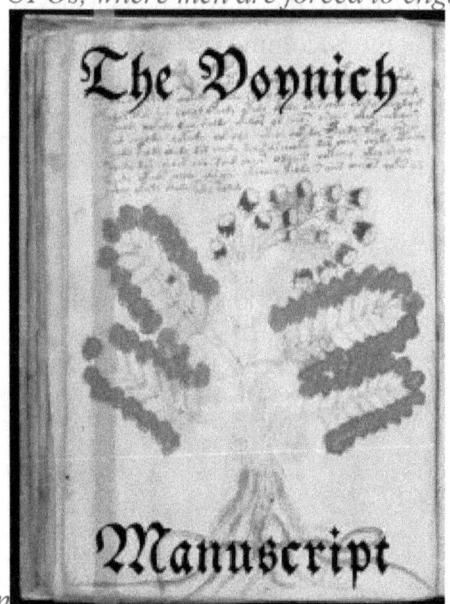

or where pregnant women have their fetus taken. What should all this have to do with each other? What do we know of fairies and what is related by the incorruptible language respectively many different languages on the subject of these fairies?

Not only are there a lot of place names, which are derived from the fairy as in Feyenoord in Holland, Sass-Fee in Switzerland or Fehndorf, Veynau, Satzvey, Burgvey, Urfey etc. in Germany. There are a huge number of words that have been received into everyday language for everyday use, which is true for all languages, without us realizing at first glance that they are dealing with the term fairy. Urfey is located near a town called Magdaberg…city of the woman or Mary. Ur means original and fey means, well, fey.

In most languages the word for fairy is being equated with the word for sorcerer or sorceress. For example, in Portuguese, the "feticero" is the wizard and the "feticera" the sorceress, both of which means fairy and these always carry a magic wand. That is , a rod, a metal rod with which they can cause electrical forces to conjure mighty things, like in the fairy tale of Sleeping Beauty, where a wicked fairy can put the entire workforce of a castle in sleep and thus override their natural defences. The same has been reported a thousands of times by people who claim to have been abducted by UFOs. The four items a fey always has: sword or dagger, wand, a book….?

Fairies are almost always dressed in white, just like the "Mary" – phenomena and the "Dames Blanches" in France and Spain. It has so deeply penetrated the language that one cannot doubt the original true state of affairs. In the English language, where fairies (Ger., 'Feen;) are "fairies", which suggests "fair" and white, blonde, as well as in Hungarian, where white "Feher" is, the "noble Fee". The old German word "her", which stands for "sublime, glorious, holy, noble" has gone out of current, bar some Christmas carols. Great Britain and Ireland are classical countries for traditional myths and legends of fairies, much more numerous than in any other country, despite the fact that there is no lack of these either. There are good and bad fairies. This fact is important to keep firmly in mind for further exploration of this theme. All of these stories from different cultural backgrounds yield four important clues. These stand out clear and unequivocal, if we consider the Irish and British mythology, the Oera Linda Chronicle, the

Voynich manuscript and take into consideration the analysis of the languages, when examining the term "fairy" in detail.

1. Fairies are always clearly associated with space travel and UFOs, particularly in conjunction with the Galaxy "OD", "ODO", "OTI" or "OT"

2. Fairies have to do with the ancestry of mankind and their origin from space. Namely, the good fairies.

3. The evil fairies have clearly to do with the centuries-old oppression of humanity.

There is some evidence, based on bardic tales and on scholarly writing from the 19th century, that the negative Fae may also have been Atlantean or Lemurian survivors, as were the positive Fae. The tales have them coming from under or over the sea to Ireland, eventually to meet the Tuatha de Danaan (positive Fae?). One wonders what could have happened to cause such a split, a fracturing, a psychosis? It does remind me of the split between the hemispheres of the brain really. However, it is also possible that these are two separate life forms. There is a life form which may have been Lemurian, may well have come from the sea somewhere between 15 and 5,000 years ago. Those who met the Formorans on the shores of Ireland, the Tuatha de Danaan, may have been Atlantean survivors, from the area of the Danube perhaps led by an entity referred to as Dana. We may well be speaking of two different beings, only one of which is the Fae.

Rock Strata.		Depth of Strata. Feet.	Races of Men.	Cataclysms.	Animals.	Plants.
Laurentian	Archilithic or Primordial	70,000	First Root Race which being Astral could leave no fossil remains.		Skull-less Animals.	Forests of gigantic Tangles and other Thallus Plants.
Cambrian						
Silurian						
Devonian	Paleolithic or Primary.	42,000	Second Root Race which was Etheric.		Fish.	Fern Forests.
Coal						
Permian						
Triassic	Mesolithic or Secondary.	15,000	Third Root Race or Lemurian.	Lemuria is said to have perished before the beginning of the Eocene age.	Reptiles.	Pine and Palm Forests.
Jurassic						
Cretaceous						
Eocene	Cenolithic or Tertiary.	5,000	Fourth Root Race or Atlantean.	The main Continent of Atlantis was destroyed in the Miocene period about	Mammals.	Forests of Deciduous Trees.
Miocene						
Pliocene						

This graph is from a book called The Lost Lemuria by Jason Colavato. It is something of a theosophical treatment of the subject of the lost civilizations. From the same book, we find a possible explanation for the good Fae: **Teachers of the Lemurian Race.** We also find a possible explanation for the bad fairies…grumpy Lemurians.

"But now there occurred an event pregnant with consequences the most momentous in the history of the human race. An event too full of mystical import, for its narration brings into view Beings who belonged to entirely different systems of evolution, and who nevertheless came at this epoch to be associated with our humanity.

The lament of the Lhas "who had not built men," at seeing their future abodes defiled, is at first sight far from intelligible. Though the descent of these Beings into human bodies is not the chief event to which we have to refer, some explanation of its cause and its result must first be attempted. **Now, we are given to understand that these Lhas were the highly evolved humanity of some system of evolution which had run its course at a period in the infinitely far-off past. They had reached a high stage of development on their chain of worlds, and since its dissolution had passed the intervening ages in the bliss of some Nirvanic condition. But their karma now necessitated a return to some field of action and of physical causes, and as they had not yet fully learnt the lesson of compassion, their temporary task now lay in becoming guides and teachers of the Lemurian race, who then required all the help and guidance they could get.**

But other Beings also took up the task--in this case voluntarily. These came from the scheme of evolution which has Venus as its one physical planet. That scheme has already reached the Seventh Round of its planets in its Fifth Manvantara; its humanity therefore stands at a far higher level than ordinary mankind on this earth has yet attained. They are "divine" while we are only "human." The Lemurians, as we have seen, were then merely on the verge of attaining true manhood. **It was to supply a temporary need--the education of our infant humanity--that these divine Beings came--as we possibly, long ages hence, may similarly be called to give a helping hand to the beings struggling up to manhood on the Jupiter or the Saturn chain. Under their guidance and influence the Lemurians rapidly advanced in mental growth. The stirring of their minds with feelings of love and reverence for those whom**

they felt to be infinitely wiser and greater than themselves naturally resulted in efforts of imitation, and so the necessary advance in mental growth was achieved which transformed the higher mental sheath into a vehicle capable of carrying over the human characteristics from life to life, thus warranting that outpouring of the Divine Life which endowed the recipient with individual immortality. As expressed in the archaic stanzas of Dzyan, "Then all men became endowed with Manas."

A great distinction, however, must be noted between the coming of the exalted Beings from the Venus scheme and that of those described as the highly evolved humanity of some previous system of evolution. The former, as we have seen, were under no karmic impulse. They came as men to live and work among them, but they were not required to assume their physical limitations, being in a position to provide appropriate vehicles for themselves.

The positions occupied by the divine beings from the Venus chain were naturally those of rulers, instructors in religion, and teachers of the arts, and it is in this latter capacity that a reference to the arts taught by them comes to our aid in the consideration of the history of this early race."

While this work does address the idea of a non-corporeal entity approaching the Lemurians who were, it seems, coming to a more solid form and probably pretty cranky about it (hence they had quite the reputation as a quarrelsome bunch), the stream seems to be Venusian. Atlanteans are of a Saturnine nature. So it seems to me that what is described here is a Lemurian race approaching Ireland from the west, from the 'water' meeting a people who are often described as Atlanteans, the Tuatha de Danaan (Dana of the Danube) and others from Spain and the Pyrenees. So which are the Fae? Both?

Are these the good fairies and the bad fairies? Back to Landmann...

4. Fairies deal with partly bizarre, weird and strange sexual incidents.

All fairies? We do realize today that mind control and fracturing of personality is achieved quite well with inappropriate forms of sexualisation. And we do wonder about the two types of Fae written about. On the other hand, there are all of the tales of changelings and baby switching and even potential FEtus removal.

In Irish mythology, fairies are called "the old people" that were driven out by the bearers of the Catholic faith. Fairies were descendants of the ancient gods and are called "Mannanon", ie "ancestors of men, of men." In Scotland they were equated with the ancient tribe of the Picts and in Wales they were the "Mamau", the mothers, the Mamas.

Recall that we just read the following passage: As expressed in the archaic stanzas of Dzyan, "Then all men became endowed with Manas."

Let's look at the old feast of "Halloween", that is to mean, as can easily be seen, the "allo fairies", ("allo-feen") the "fairies from space", ('allo' : Ger., 'All=Space, Galaxy') from the universe. This festival, which was celebrated in early November was also known as "Sam Fiun" means "seed of the fairies". Note, the word "seeds of the fairies" refers to a sexual act of fecundity. Another name was "Samhain", ('Hain' an old German word for 'woods') the "seeds Hain" (the 'seed forest') . *Christianity converted Halloween, from the feast of "Allfairies" to All Saints and All Souls Day.*

Linguistically this finds wonderful proof in the fact that the English word 'Saint' equates to 'Sankt' in German, to mean 'to sink, to come down, to descend'. Thus the word "sanc ta" , 'to sink- descend- there' became later, after the confusion of tongues, converted to "holy" in it's allegedly Latin version. So the phrase, "All sanc ta" (which originally meant that the fairies from space came down from Planet Fee, also written Phe) "All sanc tus", was rendered in the alleged Latin termed feast of "All saints". The phrase "ce phe us" ("comes from the planet Phe") today also equated with designates a star constellation or the alleged Greek god of sleep "or phe us" ("from the planet Phe in the Urall") or the name of the old city "E phe sus" ("God of 'E' darted to the planet Phe") do offer such references to us.

The Irish mythology is teeming with clues. There are the "Fe Arghus", the "arge (harsh) Fairy", whose spacecraft is the "Con Fearghus ". The "Con all" better of "Cun all" is the wedge-shaped (Allfahrzeug) space craft (Cun, Kun = wedge) and there is the phrase "Fe Arghus Fiodh Flio da" = the "arge" (harsh/bad/dark) Fairy flees to the (planet) Fe in the galaxy ODH ". Obviously the departure and return of fairies from space was always celebrated, and that not just on Halloween. The word "festival" attests to this fact. It reads: "Fee stib all", ("the fairy 'stibt' on into space," sputtering, "aufstiben" originally meaning "kicking, to fly up"). Likewise "fete" comes from fairies. The home of the fairies is "Avalon", is the "Au (watery plains) in space above". Spacecraft are called "vet, Phet", or "vehiculum, vehicle" in ancient texts . In the Ora-Linda-book it is reported that women (in Frisian "femna", in English "feme" = young woman, in French "femme") ruled the state. In this capacity they came to be known as Burgmagden (maids of the castle). City names such as Magdeburg or Magdala (near Weimar in Germany) testify to the Magdala fairy-Fe connection (Magdala = the "handmaid of the All", 'Universe'). The Bible carries many mentions of Magdalena ("magd – all – ena." – The maid beyond in space ") and religious scholars found that this does not necessarily denote the woman, who was placed as an acquaintance of Jesus in the drama of the New Testament. Hartmann von der Aue writes of the sorceress "Feimurgan", whihc broken down into a sentence suggests, the "Fei in Urgan", the fairy goes to Ur (all-space).

Not to forget the festival Samhain, which some scholars of mythology translate it as "Ancestors Night", or the "Night of the ancestors", as another example of revealing a deeper meaning when reading the words or their older context.

Now let us briefly turn to the phrase "Fee" by using linguistic analysis but limit ourselves to German, English and French in this endeavour. Whoever could protect themselves from the wand of the fairies, was "gefeit" ("invulnerable"). The word "feien" thus means to be protected from the "Fei", the fairy. In English "feign" = denotes deceptive, hypocritical, in what the (dark) fairies effected with their wands. The Portuguese "feticero" comes from the "Fe tiuschero" that is the "deceptive fairy", since with her wand she could not so much conjure up things, as to command powerfully devastating forces with her spell. The expression "Feint", the feint, the deception underlines this.

"Fetch" is a ghostly doppelganger, "feat" stands for heroism and "fear" uses that same 'fe' root and 'ar' denotes the craft.. (The Ar is the spacecraft of the Fee). The word "Fetish" denotes that the fear of deceiving the fairy has led to great veneration, of what today would be known as Stockholm syndrome. (The victim's identify with the acts/tools of the master to avoid further punishment) The old tales of all nations about fairies tell us now and again that the fairies or some evil fairies do kidnap little children, or sometimes replace them with ugly nasty children. The German language had coined the term 'wechselbalg', for this phenomenon, known as "changeling" in English, and "changelin" in French.. This event must have happened countless times throughout the centuries and across the world. Well, there are thousands of reports of abductions by UFOs, where exactly the same thing happens. Foetuses are taken from pregnant women or a male abductee would be forced into intecourse with so-called "blonde fairies" from the space craft. This prompted me to explore the meaning of the word fetus, similiarly and correctly spelled in a number of languages, and I could have not been more surprised. In addition to the old German word mentioned above, "tiuschen" = Pretend/Deceive, which often gets mentioned in connection with fairies, there is the word "tussen" – 'to swap', or in Middle High German "tuschen" again to swap. A "fe tus" therfore alludes to an exchange, possibly the interchanging of unborn children by fairies. This may have happened for thousands of years and may go on unabated until today. As our governments are supposed to protect us from harm, and keep bragging that they do just that, and at the same time deny the release of hard fact information about and the existence of UFOs, it conveys the message to the people in the know, that no effort is spared to cover up this very phenomenon. (One notes the similarity of the words

*"tiuschen" -täuschen, " tuschen "= replace and cover up).
In Norwegian fairies and elves are known as "Alfar", those
that travel out into space. (All- far/ ins All fahren). The word
changeling/wechselbalg is also rendered in other forms such
as " wechselkint " and/or " wihseling ". All means 'space'
in German, by the way.*

*Let us now turn to the evil fairies who eventually seized
power globally sometime between the 9th and 13th centuries.
This would coincide completely with the period of time which
has been called into serious question in terms of the standard
chronology. It is anything before the 9th century which
cannot be verified and anything prior to the 16th century
which cannot be depended upon as true at all. This would to
some extent explain the dismissive behaviour of officials in
governments, politicians and religious dignitaries of our
time.*

*Where do the terms serfdom and feudal rule originate from
and what do they impart?*

*In most languages, you the word is more correctly rendered
as "feodal" instead of feudal. "Fe od al" means the Planet
"Fe" in the galaxy "Od" in the "All" (Space/Universe) or it
could be the "Fee" from the galaxy "Od" in "All". Since
the planet Phecda is located within the Big Dipper or
Plough, then t he galaxy of Od is our own Milky Way Galaxy,
obviously.*

*"Feoff" in English denotes "vassal"; "fee" also denotes
genetic material, or wage payment; "feud" is the dispute, the
"feud". The revolt of the serfs against the evil lords thus led*

to the feud, to battle. Serfdom, in French "servage" (which comes very close to a meaning implying slavery) was therefore introduced by the evil Beings of the galaxy Od from the planet "Fe, Phe". Here are some interesting words in connection with the term fairy. So "felix" does not only stand for the Latin word "the lucky one" but "lix" better "Lich" stands for the planet's surface. "Fe Lich" is thus the "surface of the planet Fe." Fecundo "today means " fruitful "in many languages and suggests memories of the sexual practices described above, but" Kundo, Cundo "is the ambassador, the herald, the angel (Anglo-Saxon) the announcer/messenger from the planet Fe. In many fairy tales, fairies, goblins and gnomes were addressed "fetiro", the cousin.

A fight with fairies was "fehtan" = fencing, (German term for the sport fencing = 'Fechten'). The word vehemently" Vehemens "(Fehemens = the "Fe leads hem into the otherworldly All"), stands for energetic, vigorous, stormy during the launch process of the spaceship on its voyage "Home to the otherworldly universe". And last not least, we must not omit the word phenomenon (Phe no men); an appearance from Planet Phe, a "men" from the Planet Phe. The Russian name and surname Feodor, Fjodor, as well as the "Phoenix (Phenix, Fenix) from the ashes" are indicative of the planets Fe, Phe in the galaxy. "Phe nich, Phe tilts toward the planet Phe, since most UFO's tend to tilt sideways during the first phase of lift off.

If there is any irrefutable linguistic proof as to the true background of the fairy tale, populated by elfins and fairies the search for truth which forms the basis of this present study, it is found in the Japanese word for fairy tales:

otogibanashi, "ot (h) o gi ban ashi", for " the track/course up to the Galaxy "ot" moves the "Asch" The "Asch", the saucer, the flying saucer, the old term for UFO's. (And, as I remarked earlier, we start with the fairy tale in Steiner or Waldorf schools which is meant to be delivered to the students as a recapitulation of the epochs of humanity).

Let's gather some evidence and facts about about the mysterious galaxy " Ot, Od". The famous pyramids in Mexico are in "Teotihuacan", te oti huacan ", the" craft of the Galaxy "ot". Pyramids, the word itself says it. "Pyra miden", "fire" (pyra) and "shun" (miden; Ger: meiden). They never served as tombs for megalomaniac rulers, but as landing places for aerospace mother-ships. This is the reason why huge scorch marks feature in the upper parts of the Egyptian pyramids.

(In his landmark book, The Giza Power Plant (Bear & Co., 1998), engineer Chris Dunn made the suggestion there is evidence that the Great Pyramid may have experienced a cataclysmic event, an explosion some time in its distant past; The Translator.)

The Book of Exodus of the Bible which, incidentally and to the surprise of many, was not related to an exodus of the Jewish people from Egypt, whose existence as a religious community came much, much later. The application of linguistic analysis reads as follows: The Ex, Ech, Eck, the Kun, the device, the tri which Triex, Trieck, (triangle), these are all descriptions within ancient texts around the world, for vast triangular UFO's that are reported even today on an almost daily basis. There are particularly numerous sightings reported over the North Sea, Alaska and Canada.

"Ex od us" means, therefore, "Ex", the triangular spacecraft from the galaxy of "Ot, Od". And since "Fe" is not the only planet in this galaxy, after our month February is called we also find the planet "Sept", a term often used in Exodus as in "Septuagint", "Sept uagin ta", "uagin", waggon or "car of the planet Sept '.

In the Voynich manuscript, which had been in the hands of the Jesuits for centuries, we find a presentation of planets on 12 pages, that gave the names to the months of our calendar. However, just the very page containing important information about the planet "Fe" relating to February seem to have gone missing. The Jesuits in question seem have done "a great job", to have made this page disappear. Now, where do we locate the planet "Fe" in the galaxy "Ot"....?

By the way, the forest area of Odenwald, near Heidelberg, carries a reference to this galaxy too. Back to the investigation: After the "evil fairies" (ie aliens) had driven away the "good fairies" approximately between the 9th to 13th or 14th century, of our current falsified chronology, as already mentioned, they fostered the introduction of the alleged 3 major monotheistic religions, which are by no means 2000 years old and cannot count as real religions since linguistic analysis reveals that their sacred books are totally mistranslated. Thus, these writings began mainly to be used thereafter as powerful tools for the domination and oppression of the population. It therefore comes as no accident, for example, that the Islamist terrorist organization Alkaida is named after the star Alkaid of the Ursa Major constellation (the great bear), even if the activists involved might not know. It's sponsors and backers discretely hiding behind the scenes, on the other hand, are very likely to be fully cognizant and in the know about this supposed 'coincidence'. The word used mostly in the Voynich manuscript is "haud". The reference is the star "Al haud" located in Ursa Major, the galaxy of Ot which is just a measly 44 light-years away from us. Just outside the front door of our system, so to speak. Even the Koran, albeit another heavily doctored translation, still mentions the star Alhaud. However, it renders the name of this star as "the basin". In "Latin" texts appears the term "haud, haut" so numerously that it has been rendered as "not" rather than uppermost or high. The French language related to many European languages, is the only one that renders the word "haut" as "high".. In Irish mythology, which is teeming with the word "dubhshaoileann", which must be rendered as part of the sentence: "Dubhs hao il EA" ("to the star Dubhe of the Big Dipper high above rushes he into the galaxy) And who is he who hurries up there ? It is the hero "Cuchulain". "Cuchula", "Kugaul", "Kukul" is thiodic, or old German for "the ball", "in" is "in". Therfore, one made use of spherical spaceships to speed to the star "Dubhe".

So look at a star chart of the Ursa Major, of which the Big Dipper forms one part. At the rear to the right of the alleged dipper, is the star Dubhe, almost vertically below we find the star Alhaud, or Haud, classified by astronomers with Theta Ursa Mayor. The neighbourhood between Dubhe and Alhaud is where the fairies came from. The good "fairies" who are the "fairies" of our ancestors and our friends, and the bad "fairies" who for centuries now have used their influences to foster the secret world domination of our planet via secret societies and the practitioners of the craft. The men and women from the project "Seti "(which, by the way, was only incepted for dumbing down- and cover-up purposes) should specifically target their antennas into that drection if they do actually want to receive some extraterrestrial radio signals. However, as is abundantly clear throughout our languages, even these aliens have been here for millennia. Maybe this article should be forwarded via e-mail to the postbox of "Seti" by a few hundred people. It would be interesting to know how these people and our corporate media react or if they respond to it at all.

1https://en.wikipedia.org/wiki/Oera_Linda_Book
2https://en.wikipedia.org/wiki/Voynich_manuscript

In Steiner's treatise of the Mystery School of Ephesus, we find the following:
http://wn.rsarchive.org/Lectures/GA232/English/GC1985/19231130p01.html

(The Fae as the eyes of the earth, reflecting the cosmos back down into it). RS 'I need not mention that the stars are also there during the day only that the sunlight is of course too strong for us to perceive them. The stars do not appear by day, but if you have at any time the opportunity of going down into a deep cellar over which there is a tower over the top, then, because you are looking out of the darkness and the sunlight does not confuse you, you can see the stars even by day. I only mention this by the way to make clear to you that this reflection of the stars in the snowflakes and generally all crystals is of course present during the day. And it is not a physical reflection but a spiritual reflection. The impression one receives of this must be communicated inwardly.' The earth used to be completely at one with the universe, in the Saturn incarnation. However, it has achieved its independence now. As we go further into the earth, beyond the virginal element of say the granite in the alps to the metals beneath, (I am reminded that the chemical sign for iron is Fe and that the Fey joined with the earth much in the way that RS described the Christ joining), metals themselves can be seen as independent of the earth around them. Something quite different.

There is a supposed lineage, whether actual or whether it is merely an outline of the real toward the legend:

Danu
|
Tuatha De Danann

Nuada   **Dian Cecht**   **Dagda**

Ogma   **Brigid**   **Bres**

```
                        Daoine
                        Sidhe



Slyph      Satyr        Nymphs    Elves           Troll


Pixies     Pooka                  Dryiads   Dwarf

                    Merfolk

Sprite



                              Browines        Gnome

              Kelpie    Selkies
```

__Leprechaun__

The Sidhe are mentioned as a supernatural race in a parallel universe. However, I believe this is a medieval tale and so is suspect thanks to the revision of history in the 16th century. I believe it is more accurate to explain that there were entities who joined with the planet and entities who were chased around the planet, some call them the Survivors, were aspects of the Fae (Phe), one of if not the original seed race. They could have been the Tuatha de Danaan but medieval tales recounts earlier peoples, perhaps the Danu?

The Irish call the Ley Lines 'Fairy Paths.' Why? My research indicates that, in fact, the Fae who enmeshed themselves into the earth, wedded themselves, and act as shepherds and the eyes of the earth and guard the ley lines, as well. There is a tremendous amount of folklore and superstition, if you like, regarding the blocking of these fairy paths. In fact, there are hundreds if not thousands of catalogued incidents in which something terrible happened to someone who blocked a 'fairy path.' Often the stories are of misfortune, illness or death, especially of children. It seems rather obvious that the cause of the negative events must be traced back to the blocking of the energy of the ley lines and not to the ill will of any Fae Guardians.

"According to folklore a **fairy path** (or 'passage', 'avenue', or 'pass') is a route taken by fairies usually in a straight line and between sites of traditional significance, such as fairy forts or raths (a class of circular earthwork dating from the Iron Age ... supposedly), "airy" (eerie) mountains and hills, thorn bushes, springs, lakes, rock outcrops, and Stone Age monuments. Ley lines and spirit paths have some similarities with these fairy paths... In some parts of Ireland, Brittany and Germany there were fairy or spirit paths that while being invisible nevertheless had such perceived geographical reality in the minds of the country people that building practices were adapted to ensure they were not obstructed. A significant number of the characteristics of fairy paths are shared in common with ley lines. In many parts of Northern Europe the round barrows were the traditional homes of the fairies and were avoided by the country folk. Cornwall was and is a stronghold of fairy lore: fairies are said to dance on Carn Gluze, near St. Just in Penwith In Danish Jutland there was a belief that "Barrow-folk" dwelt in .barrows and were descendants of fallen angels cast out of Heaven. Likewise, it was considered bad luck to let cattle graze on any place where the Elf-folk have been, or to let the cattle mingle with the large blue cattle of the elves. (**Large blue cattle of the elves**?) However, all evils may be averted if one were to ask at an "Elf-barrow" for permission to graze cattle on their mounds. In Sweden, similar beliefs existed and one barrow called *Helvetesbacke* (*"Hell's mouth"*) that lies near Kråktorps gård, was claimed to be the burial mound of Odin. In Germany the Wild Troop of Rodenstein was said to ride a straight path between the castles of Rodenstein and Schnellert.

Also throughout Europe are corpse roads, which are generally believed to be of the same basic belief as *fairy paths* and most likely  share an origin. In Germany and the Netherlands in particular, these tend to be straight invisible lines and are known by a variety of names including *Geisterweg* ("ghost-way" or "ghost-road") and *Helweg* ("hell-way" or "hell-road") in German and *Doodweg* ("death-way" or "death-road") in **Dutch**. A similarly straight road did however run straight over various burial mounds at Rösaring, **Lassa** in southern Sweden... In some parts of Ireland, Brittany and Germany there were fairy or spirit paths that while being invisible nevertheless had such perceived geographical reality in the minds of the country people that building practices were adapted to ensure they were not obstructed straight path between the castles of Rodenstein and Schnellert. In Ireland, people who had illnesses or other misfortune, were said to live in houses that were "in the way" or in a "contrary place", obstructing a fairy path. An example is that of a family in which four children sickened and died, leaving the doctors baffled. The fifth child sickened and was near death, only to make a sudden and full recovery. The father told the doctor that he had consulted a wise woman who informed him that his new house extension blocked a fairy path between two fairy forts, whereupon he demolished it and his child became healthy again.[10]

An example of this fairy path straightness is provided by an account concerning a croft (now a cattle shed) at Knockeencreen, County Kerry. In an interview in the 1980s, the last human occupant told of the troubles his grandfather had experienced there, with his cattle periodically and inexplicably dying. The front door is exactly opposite the back door. The grandfather was informed by a passing gypsy that the dwelling stands on a fairy path running between two hills. The gypsy advised the grandfather to keep the doors slightly ajar at night to allow the fairies free passage. The advice was heeded and the problem ceased. It so happens that the building is indeed on a straight line drawn between two local hilltops, and is, moreover, at one end of a long, straight track.

The fairies processed from Rath Ringlestown in Ireland every night and parents brought their children in before the fairies were due to pass. The path passed round several bushes which were left undisturbed by the locals. A man who cut down one bush could not get it to burn and sickened and died within a short while as a supposed consequence of his actions. The route also passed between two mud-wall houses and a man who was out at the wrong time was found dead; the fairies having taken him for getting in the way of the procession. A traditional folk tale from the Southern Shore of Newfoundland, Canada, concerns a young married couple who discovered that they had built their house on a path used by the good people, and the steps that couple take to rid themselves of fairy mischief. It seems therefore that the fairy folk had emigrated together with their human counterparts or had been in Canada from time immemorial.

Home-owners have knocked corners from houses because the corner blocked the fairy path, and cottages have been built with the front and back doors in line, so that the owners could, in need, leave them both open and let the fairies troop through all night.

It was believed that a house built on a fairy path would suffer from midnight noises or supernatural manifestations. Ill-luck in the form of sick farm animals or personal illness could be the result and one remedy was to build small fires in several places along the fairy path, using fire from the blessed fire of Sain John's's Eve that was lit every year at sunset on 23 June... Some builders used to use a technique to see if the planned construction was going to be on a fairy path; they would map out the floor plan in the earth and place a pile of stones at each corner and leave it overnight, if the stones were undisturbed it was safe to build, otherwise the work would not continue. There is another theme that states if one's house is on a fairy path, one must leave the doors and windows open at night, front and back, to allow fairies to pass through. Builders were also advised against using white quartz in their stonework, as it is said to be a fairy stone.[17]

Wise-women were thought to be able to advise home builders of the existence of fairy paths, however in most folk-tales they are only consulted after the event and as a result of disturbances, bad luck, etc.

A building placed on a fairy path would be demolished by the fairy folk, at least twice, often remaining standing however on the third attempt... Paths that the fairies travel along are usually stated as being best avoided, however they also had certain benefits to humans, such as with 'trods' in the West of England. These are a straight-line fairy path in the grass of a field with a different shade of green to the rest. People with rheumatism sought relief by walking along these tracks, though animals avoid them. Great danger was still very much associated with using these paths at times when a supernatural procession might be using them. **Fairy rings** have certain elements in common with this phenomenon and were seen as 'gateways' into the realm of supernatural beings.[19]

The **Tylwyth teg** of Wales have paths on which it is death for a mortal to walk.[20]

The **Breton Ankou**, who is king of the dead, and his subjects have their own particular paths along which they process… Irish fairy paths are said to also exist under water, reminiscent of causeways in marshes at sacred sites and those to crannogs and other islands. These paths, only used by the fairy folk, ran from one island to another and were paved with coral, making them and their travellers visible to fishermen in their boats above.

It is my opinion that all of these stories about inexplicable consequences of crossing the paths of the fairies have only to do with interrupting the power and energy of a ley line, whose purpose and use we no longer understand.

The underwater fairy paths, ley lines, or Fae Paths, would go straight to the Battle of Moytura in which the negative entities are seen to have come from the sea, either under or over it. This would have been those who met the Fir Bolg during this battle. Then the Tuatha de Danaan arrived. 19th century scholars have placed the Formora as Atlantean remnants definitely. There is evidence to strongly suggest they were instead the transitional entities between Lemuria and Atlantis. There is ample discussion, as well, that there were, in the end, two types of Fae…one negative and one positive. Those remnants of Atlantis who were the positive Fae were chased over ther globe, hunted and exterminated by the negative Fae.

There is a wealth of evidence, as well, that the Survivors of Atlantis were with us up until a couple of centuries ago and may well still be existing without our conscious awareness..

The arrival of the Fae belongs to the old Saturn incarnation, despite some discussion of an arrival of Helper beings from Venus, and may originally have been much less material than modern humans but rather a more etheric being. The Fae must have arrived during the Saturn period of the earth's development, which would have meant they came as (started as) a less material being. There was a fire-mist era and a water-mist era. Often people refer to othewr-worldly beings as energetic. To me this means an appearance and presentation that is different enough as to appear to be non-corporeal.

Just by way of interest in ley lines and fairy paths around the world: The Aborigines of Australia tell of a '*pastage*', which they call the 'dream-time', when the 'creative gods' traversed the country and reshaped the land to conform with important paths called '*turingas*'. They say that at certain times of the year these 'turingas' are revitalised by energies flowing through them fertilising the adjacent countryside. They also say that these lines can be used to receive messages over great distances.

The Incas used 'Spirit-lines' or '*ceques*' with the Inca temple of the sun in Cuzco as their hub. The Jesuit father Bernabe Cobo referred to these '*ceques*' in his '*History of the new World*'. 1653. Alas it was my discovery in the first episode that anything written by the Jesuits and meant to represent authentic history is well nigh automatically unbelievable. However, these were lines on which '*wak'as*' were placed and which were venerated by the local people. Ceques were described as sacred pathways. The old Indian word 'ceqque' or 'ceque' means boundary or line. Cobo describes how these lines are not the same as those at Nazca, being only apparent in the alignment of the wak'as. These wak'as were most often in the form of stones, springs, and often terminating near the summits of holy mountains. Documentary records made by the Spanish record that 'qhapaq Hucha' ceremonies of human sacrifice (usually children), took place at wak'as as an annual event and also at times of disaster. In the 17th century the Roman Catholic Church ordered that the holy shrines along the routes be destroyed. Now this is very easy to believe. As in Europe, many ancient holy places were built over with churches.

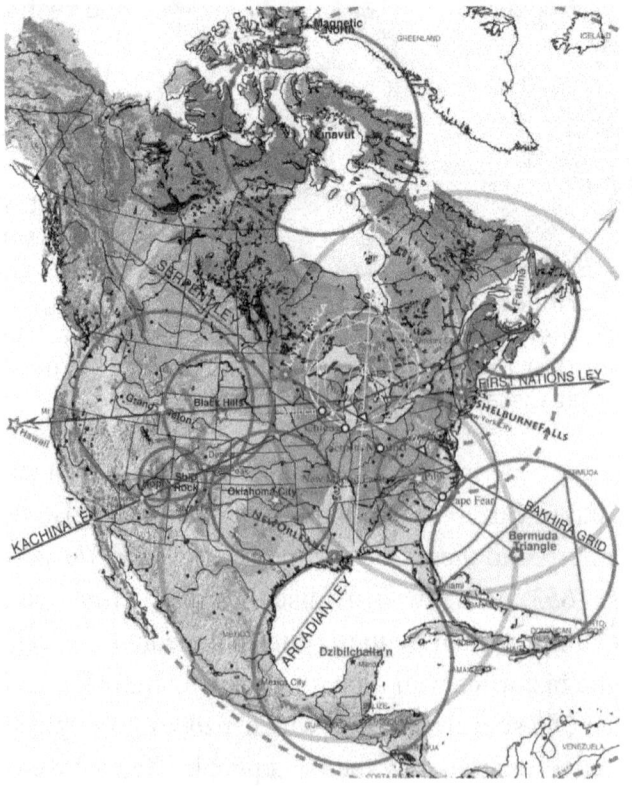

Elsewhere in America, fragments of ancient tracks can still be found such as the Mayan *'Sache'*, of which 16 have so far been found originating in Coba, Mexico. The following is a description of one found in the Yucatan;

'...a great causeway, 32ft wide, elevated from 2-8 ft above the ground, constructed of blocks of stone. It ran as far as we could follow it straight as an arrow, and almost flat as a rule. The guide told us that it extended 50 miles direct to Chichen itza*(it started from the other chief town of Coba) and that it ended at the great mound, 2km to the north of Nohku or the main temple in a great ruined building'.* (3)

Other ancient tracks have been found in New Mexico. These roads are barely visible at ground level and radiate from Chaco Canyon. They may have something to do with Orion.

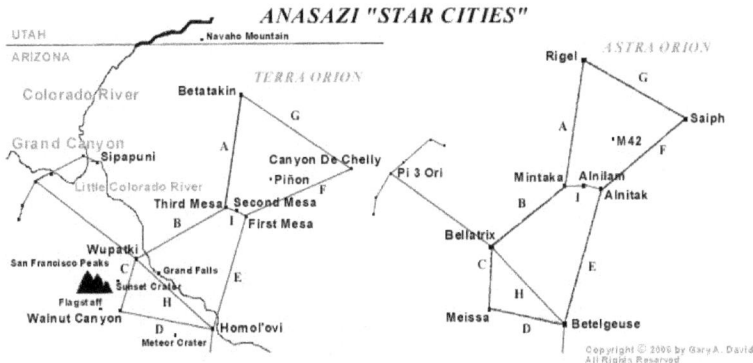

As in Bolivia, some of these paths run parallel and others lead to nowhere. One of the major sites connected by the 'Anasazi' roads is Pueblo Alto.

The German equivalent of ley lines is *'Heilige Linien'*, or 'holy lines'. The area of 'Teutberger Wald', also known as the 'German heartland' has a significant network of these lines which include the Externsteine and the megalithic stone circle at Bad Meinberg.

How old are ley lines or fairy lines? As noted with the idea that the world moved from Lemurian to Atlantean 15,000-5,000 years ago, we find the following: *Exactly how old the original straight paths were is a matter of debate. We can read of ley-lines connecting offshore beneath the English channel (1), upon which basis, Behrand concluded that these particular leys must have been marked out between 7,000 BC and 6,000 BC.*

And here we have more on the Formorans and where they came from. Who actually were the Atlanteans and what do they mean by 'ships?' The following is a very civilized account of the very musical rendition of the Battle of Moytura. Its language and visuals reflect the time in which it was written.

"We would naturally expect, in view of the geographical position of the country, to find Ireland colonized at an early day by the overflowing population of Atlantis. And, in fact, the Irish annals tell us that their island was settled *prior to the Flood*. In their oldest legends an account is given of three Spanish fishermen who were driven by contrary winds on the coast of Ireland before the Deluge. After these came the Formorians, who were led into the country prior to the Deluge by the *Lady Banbha*, or Kesair; her maiden name was h'Erni, or Berba; she was accompanied by fifty maidens and three men--Bith, Ladhra, and Fintain. Ladhra was their conductor, who was the first buried in Hibernia. That ancient book, the "Cin of Drom-Snechta," is quoted in the "Book of Ballymote" as authority for this legend.

The Irish annals speak of the Formorians as a warlike race, who, according to the "Annals of Clonmacnois," "were a sept descended from Cham, the son of Noeh, and lived by pyracie and spoile of other nations, and were in those days *very troublesome to the whole world.*"

Were not these the inhabitants of Atlantis, who, according to Plato, carried their arms to Egypt and Athens, and whose subsequent destruction has been attributed to divine vengeance invoked by their arrogance and oppressions?" sacred texts Ignatius Donnelly

The Formorians were from Atlantis. They were called *Fomhoraicc, F'omoraig Afraic*, and *Formoragh*, which has been rendered into English as *Formorians*. They possessed ships, and the uniform representation is that they came, as the name *F'omoraig Afraic* indicated, from *Africa*. But in that day Africa did not mean the continent of Africa, as we now understand it. Major Wilford, in the eighth volume of the "Asiatic Researches," has pointed out that Africa comes from *Apar, Aphar, Apara*, or *Aparica*, terms used to signify "the West," just as we now speak of the Asiatic world as "the East." When, therefore, the Formorians claimed to come from Africa, they simply meant that they came from the West--in other words, from Atlantis--for there was no other country except America west of them.

They possessed Ireland from so early a period that by some of the historians they are spoken of as the aborigines of the country.

The first invasion of Ireland, subsequent to the coming of the Formorians, was led by a chief called

Partholan: his people are known in the Irish annals as "Partholan's people." They were also probably Atlanteans. They were from Spain. A British prince, Gulguntius, or Gurmund, encountered off the Hebrides a fleet of thirty ships, filled with men and women, led by one Partholyan, who told him they were from Spain, and seeking some place to colonize. The British prince directed him to Ireland. ("De Antiq. et Orig. Cantab.")

Spain in that day was the land of the Iberians, the Basques; that is to say, the Atlanteans.

The Formorians defeated Partholan's people, killed Partholan, and drove the invaders out of the country.

The Formorians were a civilized race; they had "a fleet of sixty ships and a strong army."

The next invader of their dominions was Neimhidh; he captured one of their fortifications, but it was retaken by the Formorians under "Morc." Neimhidh was driven out of the country, and the Atlanteans continued in undisturbed possession of the island for four hundred years more. Then came the Fir-Bolgs. They conquered the whole island, and divided it into five provinces. They held possession of the country for only thirty-seven years, when they were overthrown by the Tuatha-de-Dananns, a people more advanced in civilization; so much so that when their king, Nuadha, lost his hand in battle, "Creidne, the artificer," we are told, "put a silver hand upon him, the fingers of which were capable of motion."

This great race ruled the country for one hundred and ninety-seven years: they were overthrown by an immigration from Spain, probably of Basques, or Iberians, or Atlanteans, "the sons of Milidh," or Milesius, who "possessed a large fleet and a strong army." This last invasion took place about the year 1700 B.C.; so that the invasion of Neimhidh must have occurred about the year 2334 B.C.; while we will have to assign a still earlier date for the coming of Partholan's people, and an earlier still for the occupation of the country by the Formorians from the West."

The one thing that should be amply evident is that entities known as the Fae have had a profound influence over the geography, literature and history of our human awareness. It is almost beyond the realm of possibility that these people did not exist and in great numbers. It is my contention after reading the detailed research of Erhard Landmann, that these people were a powerful and influential interstellar race and, based on the stories surrounding them and their relationships with 'ordinary' mortals they were more surely a very important seed race. Some will say the Phe still exist and still engage in human abduction. Some will say that the Fae are rising again to prtect the earth from the other, more aggressive, less compassionate and moral interstellat races. In fact, my research and my heart and my intuition tell me that all of the above are true.

Cara St.Louis - London 2016

www.ingramcontent.com/pod-product-compliance
Lightning Source LLC
Chambersburg PA
CBHW061301040426
42444CB00010B/2459